Writing Saved My Life

Tina J. Pearson

DEDICATION

This book is dedicated to Grandma Gracie, Grandma Shell, and Sade'. You all have played an important role in the writing of this book and my spiritual journey. You will forever be in my heart. RIP

FOREWORD

According to Google, to be transparent means to allow light to pass through so that objects can be distinctly seen.

In *Writing Saved My Life*, Tina J Pearson allows her testimony to be the light in the midst of darkness so that the Glory of God can be distinctly seen. She takes her readers through her life journey of trials, tribulations but most importantly triumphs allowing us to see how God's plan always prevails.

As you read through these pages there is a sense that the oil of God flows through every word. This oil is directly applied to each of us as we take in the words that God has breathed through His chosen vessel. Writing Saved My Life allows each reader to reflect, respond and be restored as we travel through each chapter.

Tina, thank you for sharing your gift with the world. Thank you for writing this book so that our secret dark places can now have the opportunity to receive His light. For where there is light there can be no darkness.

Samantha S. Gaither M.A.
Founder, The Growth Experience

Table of Contents

Trust the Process

"And we know that God causes everything to work together for the good of those who love God and are called according to his purpose for them."
-Romans 8:28 NLT

Many things happen in our lives that we may not understand. However, one thing is for sure, God has the final say. He knows the ending. It is our job to trust Him. A very wise woman once said, "No matter what it looks like, no matter what it seems like, trust God." Many times, the trials and tribulations we face seem so unbearable. A lot of times we don't understand why certain things are happening, or why things may be playing out a certain way. One thing that we can be confident in is the fact that all things work for the good of those who love the Lord (Romans 8:28). We must build on our faith and trust in God to help us make it through. It is during these times that we have to dive deeper into the Word of God, pray more and harder, and praise God in advance for the victory!

It has always been my prayer for God to use me. I am so unworthy of how much He has blessed me. I am honored that He chose me to birth this book. I pray that it touches everyone that reads it. It is my hope that my story will change someone's life, set someone free, and help someone to turn to Christ. As I share my spiritual journey with you, I hope that it blesses you. Being transparent about my life has always been a challenge. I felt I had to be "Miss Perfect." That's how I know this is all God. I would have never done it by choice.

Tina J. Pearson

My Prayer

Lord I thank you for everyone reading this book. I thank you for allowing me to use my story for your glory. I thank you for the trials and tribulations that we face. They provide us with a testimony to help others. I thank you for the mindset shift that is going to come upon everyone that reads this book. I thank you for the spiritual growth for everyone that reads this book. I ask that You bless everyone that comes in contact with my story. Let this be a tool to catapult them to tell their story. I pray my story will help someone else continue to push, to pray, to war. I pray that this book will draw someone closer to You. I pray this book will change the atmospheres in which it enters. I pray this book will help someone to gain knowledge and wisdom along their spiritual journey. I ask for a special blessing for everyone that reads this book. I ask that You provide the needs of your people, bring about breakthroughs, bring about healing, make every crooked path straight, and show us the purpose of our lives. I pray You will continue to use us as Your vessels and Your voice in the Earth. I pray You will help us to see things through our spiritual lens. I thank you for our journeys, and I pray that we will all continue to grow closer to You.

In Jesus' Name,

Amen

Before I Knew God

"Then Jesus said, "Come to me, all of you who are weary and carry heavy burdens, and I will give you rest. Take my yoke upon you. Let me teach you, because I am humble and gentle at heart, and you will find rest for your souls. For my yoke is easy to bear, and the burden I give you is light." -Matthew 11:28-30 NLT

"Behold, I stand at the door and knock; if anyone hears My voice and opens the door, I will come into him and will dine with him, and he with Me." -Revelation 3:20 NKJV

I've gone through 2 cycles of depression, and I know without a doubt it was no one or nothing but God that brought me through them. Of course, I did not realize it at the time because I did not have a deep relationship with God. The crazy thing is, I thought I knew God. Sure, I had been saved and baptized; I prayed daily and read my Bible periodically. The issue was I knew God through the thoughts and opinions of other people. I knew what my momma thought about God, I knew what my daddy thought about God, I knew what my pastor(s) thought and said about God, but I did not have an opinion of my own. I did not have that tight relationship with God where He could speak to me and only me about what I was to do in my life. I was young when I decided to dedicate my life to Christ and get baptized. I did it because it was the right thing to do. I wanted a Christian filled life, but I did not fully understand all it entailed. I did not know explicitly what the Bible said. I led my life by what I was told, not by what I knew from studying the Word.

The first time I went through a depression was after the death of my maternal grandmother. I was attending college at Winthrop University. I had never lost anyone that close to me, and now that I reflect on the situation, I realize that God was preparing me for it all along. I can remember thinking and speaking throughout the year, "I don't know what I would do without my grandmother." It was December of 2005 when she passed. I was finishing my final examinations and I received that dreadful phone call while having dinner with friends.

I was in ultimate disbelief. I remember walking into the restroom at Texas Roadhouse because I could not hear my cousin on the phone. "Tina, what I am about to say is really going to hurt you." In my mind she was about to tell me something that I would really let roll off my back. "Your grandmother passed." Those words were not clear to me at first. I laughed it off and did not really believe it. If my grandmother really had passed, why did I not receive a phone call from my mom or dad? Why hadn't I heard from any of my siblings? Why did none of my aunts or uncles call me? There was no way my grandmother was dead, and no one called to inform me.

"My cousin just told me my grandmother died." Those were the words I said to my friends when I came out of the restroom. I went back to the table to sit down to eat, but I could not shake the fact that I was just told my grandmother was gone. I looked at my phone, but I still did not have a call from anyone in my family. I decided to go outside and call my mom. I remember the phone ringing and her picking up. I was so out of it; I didn't hear the sadness in her voice. "Ma, Denisha called me and told me Grandma passed. What is she talking about?" Complete silence. "Tina, Grandma is gone." At that point, my entire world stood still. I felt as if I was stuck in a bad dream. "Ma, no Ma!" "No Ma!" I could hear myself getting louder as the tears began to flow. How was this even possible? How could God take away the glue that held our family together? What was I going to do without my grandmother?

My depression did not begin until after her funeral. I do not think I realized I was going through a depression until the death of my best friend not even a year later. Her death also hit close to home. Before then, I think I thought nineteen-year-olds were invincible. Death was not a factor I dwelled upon, but at that moment I remember not wanting to live. I could not go by her family's house to visit. I couldn't even bring myself to attend her funeral.

For months I thought she was mad at me. In the wake of my depression, she came to me in a dream and told me that she was not mad at me. She also told me not to be afraid to die. Even though I felt like I wanted to die, I was very afraid of death. I would cry all the time and beg God to take the pain away. He was my only source of strength. I was such a miserable person, but I hid it well. No one knew what I was going through. I never talked to anyone in my family about it. I put on my poker face, and I was there for everyone else because that was what they needed.

On most days I did not want to get out of bed. That was the one place where I did not have to face reality. I can recall a time where I went to dinner at Chick-fil-a with my suitemates. Everyone was having a great time talking and laughing, and I was trying to fake it. The feeling that stuck with me during my depression is one I cannot describe. I felt sick. I felt this nagging heaviness, and that night it got the best of me. Amid the laughs and reminiscing of good times, I burst into tears. Because no one could know what I was dealing with, I simply acted as if I did not know what was wrong with me when my suitemates asked what was going on. Why wasn't I able to tell anyone I was going through a depression? Because I had to be Miss Perfect, and Miss Perfect has no issues. We will get to that later. I put myself last, and as a result, I did not have anyone who I could talk to about what I was going through. The one person I confided in simply told me that I needed to "get myself together." At that point I chose to lean on nothing but God. That played a major part in my spiritual growth. My relationship with God grew, and when I finally reached the light at the end of the tunnel, my life was forever changed. For a few years afterward, I would find myself trying to slip back into a depression around the anniversary of my grandmother's passing. Those were times where I had to cling to God.

"Trust in the Lord with all your heart; do not depend on your own understanding. Seek his will in all you do, and he will show you which path to take." -**Proverbs 3:5-6 NLT**

"Some people come into your life for a season and others for a lifetime. Our hearts become broken, and our vision blurred when we attempt to make seasonal people lifetime participants. Clearly, some people come into our lives for a period of time to accomplish a specific task for which we want an amiable relationship. But we cannot make a permanent investment into a temporary circumstance.

Relationships can be one of the greatest equitable assets of any individual, so how do we learn how to decide who is in and who is out? Like the pro scout, the CEO, or the wise mother, how do you delegate the right person to the right place so that we can decide how to run the team most effectively?" -T.D. Jakes, *Before You Do*

My second state of depression happened the summer of 2017, a little less than a year of me writing this. This was caused by me not trusting the process and making my own plans. God has a plan for our lives. We can choose to make our own life plans, but we set ourselves up for disappointment by doing so. My plan was to be married at the age of twenty-three, have my first child at the age of twenty-five and have my second child by the age of twenty-seven. I even planned to have my boy first, then my girl. I am sure God laughed at me. Here I am thirty-two and none of that has come to pass.

When I turned thirty, I went into panic mode. How was it possible for me to be thirty, single, with no kids? When I finally decided to date again, I just knew he was the one. I went back to being a planner. I planned out my life with this guy; I even planned to pack up my entire life to move where he was. God laughed at me again. Because I prayed for my next relationship to be my last, I knew this was it. However, God did not tell me to get into that relationship. I made the decision to do so. I then had to deal with consequences.

Sixteen. That is how old I was when I first met him. For some reason, I really was not interested in him then. To be honest, I was not interested in dating at all. I remember the day I met him. I was working at Wendy's. He came through the drive thru, and I did not pay much attention to him. The next thing I knew, he came back to the window and told me how he noticed me looking at him and asked for my number. I did not have a clue what he was talking about. Somehow, someway, we ended up talking and I eventually gave him my number. We would talk every now and then. Once I got into a relationship, our conversations came to an end. We kept in touch over the next ten years, but I still did not give him much attention.

Because I had been praying for my next relationship to be my last, I knew it was meant to be once he reentered my life. It was Memorial

Day weekend. I was already down because my brother introduced me to a guy that I had been talking to for some months. He lived about five hours away, so our entire relationship was through FaceTime. He decided to come pay me a visit that weekend. It was the first time we met. We had a great time laughing and talking that night, but the next day, he decided to go visit his friends. I was in total disbelief. Here is a guy that has been talking about a future with me, just meeting me, and now going to spend time with his friends? Was it because I did not have sex with him? I was completely taken aback.

When he actually left, I thought he was playing a joke. However, I did not hear from him the rest of the day, or the weekend. So, when this guy from my past called me, I knew it was the stars aligning. We caught up and he asked if he could come to see me. I could not believe it. I had not spoken to him in years, but he was willing to drive two hours just to spend the day with me. We went to lunch, then back to my place to catch up. I felt an instant connection. It was almost like we picked up where we left off, except this time, I was really interested.

After a few months, we decided to make it official. Did I pray about it? No. Did I listen for God's voice and guidance? No. I just jumped into the relationship. Since I was praying for my next relationship to be my last, I knew this was it. Everything started out great! He was very sweet, and he took great care of me. He never allowed me to pay for anything and he bought me any and everything I wanted. I especially loved how I would be surprised with flowers or one of my favorite things. He always made plans with "us" in mind. Everything seemed perfect!

There was a problem though, a major problem. I was the first girl he dated after separating from his daughter's mom. Until now, they still acted as a family unit. Until now, he did not have to worry about his daughter's reaction to another woman being a part of his and her lives. Initially, I was very lenient. I imagined this was a difficult situation, but as time passed, nothing seemed to change. He just did not know how to draw the line. I was not okay with Mommy and Daddy still going to dinner together and having family outings, especially since she did not even know I existed.

Don't get me wrong, I thought it was great that they could co-parent in that manner, but if I was the woman he was planning to spend forever with, I was not understanding what was so hard about introducing me to his daughter. I even pretended I was an old friend once when I ran into them together. I still cannot believe I did that. When the time came where I was completely fed up with it, he stopped talking to me. One minute we were talking about how to fix things and make them work, and the next minute I was being ignored. He did not even respond to my text messages. I could not believe my world was tumbling down again.

Due to the fact that I was blindsided by everything, I let the enemy get into my mind, and I found myself slipping back into a depression. I started questioning what was wrong with me. What was I doing wrong? Why couldn't I just be with the man God created for me? Why was I going through all of this?

Prior to this relationship, I was in a ten-year relationship, but I did not have a relationship to last longer than six months after that. I let the enemy tell me I was not good enough. I let the enemy tell me I was never going to find the man God had for me, my Boaz. I let the enemy tell me I was never going to have children. Worst of all, I let the enemy tell me that I would never have true happiness because I would never have any of those things.

Up to this point, I have failed to mention that I have four jobs. I am a middle school English language arts teacher, a Zumba instructor, a cashier at Lowes, and the owner of The Wreath Ministry. In eight years of education, I have never taken a summer off. I normally work five

18

days at Lowes, eight hours a day, and teach Zumba classes at least twice a week. After realizing how much my depression had taken over my joy and prevented me from spending time with God, I decided to do just that. I took the summer off.

It was my goal to take back my joy and get closer to God, and that was what I did. The way I grew spiritually was amazing! I spent many days on the couch reading my Bible. I had many rides in the car just talking to God. I became an active member of the illustrious group, Women Who War, that was founded by the amazing Minister Adrienne Young. I became surrounded with so many wonderful people of God. My spirituality was catapulted to the next level. I finally got to that place of peace.

July of 2017 was the month I decided to pick myself up and move on with my life. The enemy was no longer able to attack my mind. My amazing sister in Christ, Prophetess Samantha Gaither, covered Women Who War with declarations the entire month. Each declaration spoke to me. Each declaration gave me greater clarity of my situation. Each declaration gave me hope, peace, and joy. I finally got to the point of accepting the process.

The first declaration was about rest. According to Joyce Meyers, rest in God "is not a rest *from* work—it's a rest *in* work. It's partnering with God to do what He is calling you to do by His grace and leaving the part you can't do in His hands, trusting Him to do it. Hebrews 4:3 says it this way: *"For we who have believed enter that rest…* So, we start by believing."

"Come to me, all you who are weary and burdened, and I will give you rest. Take my yoke upon you and learn from me, for I am gentle and humble in heart and you will find rest for your souls. For my yoke is easy and my burden is light." -**Matthew 11:28-30 NKJV**

This declaration was the beginning of a new mindset for me. I remember thanking God for rest. I was so tired of how I was feeling. I was so tired of being unhappy, frustrated, and confused. I declared and decreed that I would have rest. I started to feel the weight life.

Day two centered around restoration. I knew at this point that God was using her to speak directly to me. I needed my joy to be restored. I needed my peace to be restored. I needed my happiness to be restored, and if I am going to be honest, I needed my faith to be restored.

"Though you have made me see troubles, many and bitter, you will restore my life again, from the depths of the earth, you will again bring me up. You will increase my honor and comfort me once more." -**Psalm 71:20-21 NIV**

In this declaration, Prophetess Samantha stated, "I declare and decree that he is restoring the years the canker worm tried to destroy." Once again, I felt a weight lifted. It is amazing how God restores what has been once taken. I could feel the joy I once had slowly begin to reenter my life. It was a feeling I cannot describe. I was finally beginning to feel at peace about the situation.

The next day was about healing. At first, I did not think it applied to me. Immediately when I heard the word healing, I thought about sickness. I needed to be healed though. I needed to know that I was good enough. I needed to know that my relationship did not fail because of something being wrong with me. At this point, I finally accepted the fact that my failed relationship was a product of me not waiting on God. Once again, God used Prophetess Samantha to speak to me. A part of her declaration stated, "I declare and decree that I am healed. I declare and decree that not only am I healed, but I am also ready to forgive those that hurt me." This totally set me free. At that moment I knew I had to forgive and let it go. I stopped holding on to hope, and I was in a better headspace.

Day four, Independence Day, the day of freedom. These were the exact words I wrote in my journal...

The Bible says, "Who the son sets free, is free indeed." I declare and decree that I am free today from whatever has had me bound. God is releasing a praise in my spirit like never before! Free from FRUSTRATION!

At that point, I made a conscious decision that I would no longer be frustrated by my situation. I was far from being over everything, and I was still going through my depression, but I was getting to a point of peace.

"And the peace of God which transcends all understanding, will guard your hearts and your minds in Christ Jesus." **-Philippians 4:7 NIV**

The word transcends means to go beyond understanding. Being at peace in a situation is sometimes hard to understand and explain. I had a conversation with my brother about how I found peace, but my only explanation for how I got to that point was God. I did not think it was by happenstance that peace was the topic for the fifth day. There is no peace like peace given by God. Amid my storm, God gave me peace. I did not know how I was going to get through. I wanted to see the light at the end of the tunnel. I wanted everything to be over so that I could go back to the happy person I was used to being, but I finally found peace. Things were slowly getting better.

Throughout the remainder of the month, God continued to speak to me. I was so in love with how much I was drawing nearer to Him. On day six I declared and decreed that God would give me strength to face every obstacle in my life. I declared and decreed that I would have peace of mind on day nine. Authority is what I declared and decreed over my situation on day twelve, and on day fourteen I declared and decreed that I was enough. Day sixteen was a Sunday. I went to church that morning, and once again, I knew God was speaking to me. Some of the things said by Pastor Price were:

"Sometimes we go through things to let us know where we are." As I reflected on this, I felt like I was going through this depression to get closer to God.

"It doesn't matter where I'm at in the race, all that matters is that I win! I have a course and a race to run. I am going to finish my race. I'm going to fight and keep the faith because the Lord has a crown of righteousness for me." At this point in his sermon, I knew I had to continue to press forward. I was tired. I longed for the day when I would finally be back to normal, but I also knew I could not quit.

My journal for that day turned out to have a different outcome from what I expected. It said,

07/16/17

Today I decided to be obedient. As I was watching the Remnant Warriors Bible study video on fasting, God told me to fast for one day for him. He says he's broken. I wasn't sure if I was doing the right thing, but I received confirmation twice today. God you are so amazing! I thank You for working it out. Pastor Price said, 'sometimes you have to be a certain way so that you can show us who you are.' My sister Samantha said to press forward. 'We should not be believing in right now. We are believing to where we are going.' I just thank you Lord for where I'm going. I thank you Lord for the miracles that are about to take place in my life. I cannot thank you enough. Glory be to thy name. HALLELUJAH!

As I sit on my front porch, I can just feel the presence of the Lord. He's working it all out! Glory be to God!

One Sunday while attending my childhood church, the minister said something that stuck out to me. Even though I felt like I was drowning in my sorrow yet again, I had a little more hope this time. I knew how to trust God. Her words were, "No matter what it looks like, no matter what it seems like, trust God." She was speaking directly to me. I needed that reminder. My life was not over because things had not gone the way I planned. I am not the one in control of the plans of my life anyway. Once I realized that, I was able to trust the process.

I came out of the situation with more clarity of how a relationship should work. After months of reflection, I realized that I lowered my worth. I lowered my standards and value because I wanted to be married. I had to do whatever I needed to do to keep my man happy. That included having pre-marital sex. Well, God set me straight. I made the decision that whomever God had for me to spend the remainder of my life with was going to have to accept me for me. They would also have to accept the fact that I was not having sex before marriage. I took my wants and desires to God in prayer, and I must say I look at things differently. It's almost like God completely erased lust from my life. No more would I accept things I shouldn't. No more would I put myself second. No more would I compromise my beliefs to make a man happy.

Lord, Please Restore My Joy

*"Though you have made me see troubles, many and bitter, you will restore my life again; bring me up. You will increase my honor and comfort me once more." -***Psalm 71:20-21 NIV**

10/09/17

Lately I have been letting things of the world take my joy. I've been stressed out about this situation with my HOA, I've been frustrated because I've met a wonderful guy, but I can't move forward with him, and I've been feeling like God hasn't been hearing me. Even though I know that is not the case, I still think it. Lord I pray that You will restore my joy. The enemy has no power here. You are Almighty and You have all power in Your hands. I'm thanking you in advance for working it out.

Amen.

So, not only am I dealing with being depressed, I get a letter in the mail from a collections agency saying I owe over $2,000 because of missed HOA payments. That indeed was true. I had been paying what I could on my HOA, but it was definitely not the $155 per month they expected. I really do not know why I let this get to me as much as I did. The reason for my HOA missed payments was due to a mix up in my escrow payments with my mortgage. I was having to pay almost $300 extra each month to pay back a $2,500 difference. The problem was that I forgot to turn in my paperwork that would change my state taxes from North Carolina taxes to South Carolina taxes. During that twenty-four-month period, God always provided. Not only did it get paid back in full, but I also got a refund check for the overage I paid once I submitted my paperwork. Why did I let this situation get to me? Because I needed to be restored. I needed to get back to the place in God where my faith overpowered everything. I needed to let go of trying to fix my own brokenness and let God restore me.

What is restoration?

According to 1 Peter 5:10, restoration is when God makes you "strong, firm and steadfast." While we are in our sufferings, we are weak. We will let anything get to us. We will make a big deal out of nothing, but we must learn what weapons we need to use in every battle. Sometimes we must change our armor. What worked last time may not work this time. We must constantly be in communication with God, praising and going about our day like nothing is wrong. We must always confuse the enemy. It took me a while to learn that. As a teacher, I am constantly having to provide my students with strategies to help them master the skills and concepts I teach. If one strategy does not work, I provide them with another strategy. What works can differ from each class, or each student. One thing is for certain, if the strategy is not effective, it is a waste of time. We must think about our trials in life in the same manner. If we keep doing the same things the same way, what will change? If your old strategies are not working, why would you continue to use them? Once I learned that I needed to change my strategy, my weapons, and my armor, my joy was restored.

10/22/17

When I say I got exactly what I needed to make it through the rest of the year! Friday's prayer gathering in Greenville was such a blessing. I received so many prophecies for my life. I clearly heard from God and was able to give a Word to one of my best friends! I have no clue what God is about to do in my life, but I am so excited! The worries I have had are no longer worries. I AM THE ONE! I'm claiming to be debt free. I'm speaking God's promises into existence.

Know God for Yourself

"All Scripture is inspired by God and is useful to teach us what is true and to make us realize what is wrong in our lives. It corrects us when we are wrong and teaches us to do what is right. God uses it to prepare and equip his people to do every good work." -**2 Timothy 3:16-17 NLT**

Having a personal relationship with God is imperative to spiritual growth. You have to be able to clearly hear from Him, and you have to know Him for yourself. There was once a time I knew God through other people. I went to church every Sunday, I read my Bible periodically, I prayed constantly, but my thoughts, opinions, and beliefs were based on the thoughts, opinions, and beliefs of my pastor, my family, my friends, and other people whom I came in contact with to talk about God. That's not how God wants to be acquainted with us. I can honestly say by developing my own personal relationship with God, I view everything differently.

Growing up in a Baptist church, I felt like I was always told what was wrong. "God doesn't like this," "God frowns upon that." It seemed as if no one could make it into Heaven if they were not perfect. As I got older, I became very judgmental and forgot one thing that I believe a lot of us forget – sin is sin in God's eyes. It does not matter if it is as major as murder or as minor as a negative thought. It is still a sin. I often forgot that I had no right to judge. I thought that because I was aiming to be so perfect, the "small" sins I committed were not as bad as the "big" sins other people were committing.

Even though my relationship with God was growing stronger, I still had a lot of growing to do. It was not until the summer of 2017 that I began to realize the importance of knowing God for yourself. I spent many hours on my couch reading the Bible, praying, and talking to God, listening to inspirational messages and sermons, and fasting. Once I began to hear from God, my entire outlook on life changed. Our relationships with God are personal. They are unique to us as individuals. Yes, He created us in His own image, but He also made us all different. Think about it, are any of your relationships exactly the same? Do you communicate with everyone in your life in the same manner? I know I do not. Our relationship with God is the same way. What He gives to me, He may not give to you. What He reveals to me, may not be revealed to others. It does not mean He loves me more or you less. It means He has something else for you. What He speaks to me, He may not speak to you. Once you develop your own relationship with God, you can clearly hear from Him. You can decipher between the thoughts and opinions of others because you know what it says in His Word. You have a deeper understanding of what His Word means, and you view things through a spiritual lens.

Reading and studying the Bible is essential in your relationship with God. If you are not following His commands, you are not fully pleasing Him. You are separating yourself from Him. If you do not know what He commands, you cannot please Him. Personally, after my relationship with God grew to a personal level, things in the Bible began to make more sense. I realized before I was reading the Bible, but that was it. I did not fully understand what I was reading. Now when I read, it seems like everything is made clear. I have a deeper understanding of what God expects of me, what He has promised me, and how much He loves me. I have read the story of Adam and Eve several times, but the most recent time I read it was different. As I was reading, I placed myself in their shoes. I remember thinking, *How amazing it must have been to be in the presence of God... to be able to physically walk with God.* I never paid attention to the fact that Adam and Eve actually walked with God. They hid from Him because they could actually see Him!

> *"Your word is a lamp to my feet and a light to my path."*
> **-Psalm 119:105 NKJV**

Having a personal relationship with God also changes your perspective of what others think of you. It helps you to not try to please others, because at the end of the day, the only one we need to please is God. I can say that I have been delivered from people. Trying to be "Miss Perfect" is no longer something I desire to do. I was so caught up in trying to be the person everyone else thought I should be, I did not know who I was.

When I was finally delivered, I literally had to take time to figure out who I was and what I wanted. As long as God is satisfied with me, nothing else matters. That sounds easy, but it is not. Not everyone is going to understand why you are doing the things you are doing. Not everyone is going to view things the way you view them, and that is ok. That is why some people may only be in your life for a season. What God gives me is for me. No matter the turmoil I may have to endure, it is mine! He gave it to me for a reason. It is not for anyone else to understand.

When I was in college, my grandmother would always buy me snacks. Every time I came home, she would have a bundle of snacks waiting for me. She would also sneak and give me money. "This is for you

Punky. Don't tell anyone I gave it to you." She did not do that for anyone else. For whatever reason, God led her to bless me in that manner. It was for me and no one else.

> *"You must not covet your neighbor's house. You must not covet your neighbor's wife, male or female servant, ox or donkey, or anything else that belongs to your neighbor." -***Exodus 20:17 NLT**

That brings me to yet another great thing about having a personal relationship with God. Jealousy and envy do not exist. You could care less about what other people have. The Bible tells us not to covet, and when you know God personally, you don't. Why? Because you know He provides all of your needs, and not only will He give you want you need, but He will give you what you want. There is something about the way your faith increases when you have a personal relationship with God. You trust Him fully. You know that He will not withhold any good thing from you, so you do not worry about how He is blessing those around you, because you know your blessings are one the way. You celebrate with them because you know how blessed you are, and you are content with what God has already given you. You are happy to see those around you getting blessed as well.

Once you develop a personal relationship with God, you study and meditate on His Word, and you understand what it is saying, your thoughts and actions change. The Word becomes embedded in your mind, heart, and soul. It becomes a part of your lifestyle. It helps to guide you.

For example, growing up, my aunt always told me to never want what someone else had and to never want to be like someone else. I do not know if she was referring to one of the commandments in the Bible, but at the time, I did not even know it was a commandment in the

Bible. Now that I know, it resonates with me. I do not covet anything that God has blessed someone with because I have my own blessings. I have no need to wish for things I do not have because I know that God blesses me with things I have asked for, as well as things I have not asked for. God has blessed me abundantly, and I have no need to wish for the things that others have.

God's Timing is Perfect

"So humble yourselves under the mighty power of God, and at the right time he will lift you up in honor. Give all your worries and cares to God, for he cares about you." -1 Peter 5:6-7 NLT

Today instant gratification is what we seek. Technology has made everything easier and quicker to obtain. You don't have to leave your house to do so many things now. Grocery shopping can be done online, seeing a loved one that is miles away can be done through FaceTime and other video apps. You can even send money to someone without going to the bank. All of these things are great, but even though God can operate suddenly, that is not always the case. I have always heard the saying, "Patience is a virtue." That is true. One of the biggest lessons I have learned is how to be patient and wait on God.

Dr. James W. Goll, President of God Encounters Ministries made a very valid point in one his books, *Hearing God's Voice Today:*

The Trap of Missed Timing

There is a *kairos* moment (perfect timing) for all things. If we talk about our word too soon, we might miss the Savior's timing and end up attempting to fulfill our word with second-rate results. We should remember what happened to Abraham and not birth an Ishmael because we just *could not wait* for an Issac.

I wish I had read this and understood it years ago. I would have saved myself a lot of trouble. I have come to realize that a lot of the decisions I made were based on what I wanted for my life. God granted me the things I wanted, but in the end, it was to show me that He has something better in store for me!

I always knew that I wanted to be a teacher. I never thought it would be difficult for me to get a job. Teaching is a profession that always has job openings. However, the year I graduated was the year South Carolina's school districts went on a hiring freeze. I just knew I would have a job once I graduated. The school district for which I was completing my internship was building new schools. The school district sent me an application that I completed instantly. The assistant principal at the school where I was interning came in to observe me to see if I was a potential fit for one of the new schools where he would become the principal, and in my mind, if that did not work out, I could take the place of my mentor teacher since she was transferring to one of the new schools.

I had it all planned out. Everything was going to work out great! Boy, was I wrong! Towards the end of my internship, we had a faculty meeting. In the meeting it was announced that due to state-wide budget cuts, the district would not be hiring any new teachers. They would be on a hiring freeze. I was devastated. How could this be happening? Soon after that, as I was working at Lowe's (my part-time job throughout college), the principal from the school where I completed my field experience came through my line to check out. She asked if I had found a job and told me she would have some teacher assistant positions open. She said she realized it was not a classroom position, but it was a way to get my foot in the door.

After praying about it, I decided to take her up on her offer. Notice I said praying about it, but I said nothing about waiting on God to respond. Nonetheless, I was glad I did! After my interview, her words to me were, "You should have graduated last year." We both laughed at that. "No, but seriously, if you were my daughter, I would tell you to take this position." I took her up on her offer, and immediately fell in love with the school. Everyone was so welcoming, and the students were so sweet. I went from being the fifth-grade assistant to teaching Corrective Reading to small groups all within a year.

Being able to teach gave me so much joy and excitement! I am a very shy person (well, I used to be), but teaching gave me a rush. I loved seeing the improvements in my students with their reading capabilities. My principal instantly got me into different trainings and professional developments that would help me to grow as a teacher. She even gave me the opportunity to complete a long-term substitute position. Not only did I gain experience, but I finally got paid on a teacher salary scale for those few months. I was excited about the upcoming school year because I knew I was finally going to be a teacher! I was finally going to have my dream job and have the opportunity to make a difference in the lives of all my students! Then came another faculty meeting.

My principal had been informed that she was going to be transferred to the district office, but the good news was that my assistant principal became my new principal. I got offered a job for the following school year, but the problem was that I was not certified to teach that grade level. With that being said, I watched someone else get the job I wanted. I remained positive throughout the school year in hopes that

I would have a job the next year. I was able to teach small group reading and math. I made the most of it. I learned a lot about myself as a teacher; things that Winthrop University could not teach me. That is not taking a shot at Winthrop. I was well prepared for the classroom based on what I learned there, but there are some things we can only learn from experience. I was never more ready to be a classroom teacher.

The end of the school year came around, and once again I watched someone else get the job I felt should have been mine. At this point, I felt defeated. I could not understand why God would allow this to happen. Here it was three years later, and I still did not have my own classroom. I had no idea how I was going to make it through the new school year. That summer was hard. I applied for several jobs, but I got nothing. I finally made the decision to look outside of my current school district. Looking back at things, maybe God was trying to show me that being a teacher was not His plan for my life. I was so caught up in making my own plans, I did not think about it that way. He knew how badly I wanted to be a teacher. God is so loving that sometimes He will give us the desires of our hearts, even though it is not His desire for our lives. The good thing about that is He still brings us back to where we need to be.

"For I know the plans I have for you," says the Lord. They are plans for good and not for disaster, to give you a future and a hope." - **Jeremiah 29:11 NLT**

Somehow, I ran across a posting for a middle school reading interventionist. Initially, I did not apply for it. I had taught reading to small groups for the past three years, but I had never taught middle school. I'm sure I looked at the job posting about five times before finally applying. I got a phone call that same day, and the principal wanted me to come in as soon as possible for an interview. My interview lasted about an hour and a half. I was able to confidently talk about everything I had learned from my current position. I could tell I made a lasting impression, and I surprised myself hearing out loud how much I had learned. After waiting several long weeks, I received a phone call and was offered the job! I was filled with so many mixed emotions, but it was all in God's timing.

Was I patient throughout the process? Absolutely not! There were many times I found myself in tears because I did not have the job I wanted. There were many times I found myself questioning why God was overlooking me. The situation helped me come to the realization that I was a very impatient person. This was my first true test of being patient, waiting on God, and trusting His timing and plan for my life, and I failed miserably. Had I not gotten the three years of experience I received by accepting the position as a teacher assistant, I would not have been prepared to be a reading interventionist.

My first day was a nightmare! I fought hard to hold back the tears, and I did not want to go back to work. There were a lot of materials for me to use, but I was not familiar with any of them. Unlike Corrective Reading that was scripted, I had nothing to go by. Adjusting to middle school students was also hard. I was used to just giving my elementary babies that "teacher look" and they would get back on task. That did not work in middle school.

Thank goodness for mentors. Had it not been for my mentor, and now good friend Shanell, my first year with my own classes would have been a disaster. She taught me the skills needed to handle middle school kids. Because I went through extensive training in Corrective Reading, I, with the help of the other reading interventionist, and of course God, was able to create the curriculum for the course. That brings me to yet another blessing from this situation.

Upon hiring me, my new principal asked me for recommendations for the second reading interventionist. He told me none of the candidates he interviewed rose to my standards. While at my old job, I met a wonderful lady that was also trying to enter the teaching field as well. She was substitute teaching in hopes of receiving a job. We became great friends during that time, and she was hired after her interview. We worked closely together, and I learned a lot from her. So, with all this wonderful stuff happening, it could be possible that I was fulfilling the purpose and plan God had for my life, right? Everything was finally falling into place. Life was grand! I was happy to finally have the only job I have ever wanted. I would often say, "If I don't teach, I may be a bum on the street because I have no clue what else I want to do with my life." Notice "I" was the one making the plans.

The following year I was offered a position as a literacy coach. The interesting part about that was I was working on my master's degree in literacy to be a literacy teacher and literacy coach. That was also a wonderful experience. I must say I was a little concerned with the fact that I had technically been a classroom teacher for a year. My principal assured me that he had full confidence in me. I was glad for the opportunity because I had planned to become a literacy coach after teaching for a few years. I knew I wanted to get my master's degree in literacy before graduating with my undergraduate degree. One of my professors whom I admire suggested I go that route being able to have that position without applying, interviewing, even inquiring about it was mind blowing. And it came at the perfect time. This had to be God's next step in the plan for my life!

I was able to learn things from my classes from my master's program and put them into practice shortly after. I was very appreciative of the openness and reception of my colleagues, considering the fact that I had only been at the school for one year, and I had less classroom experience than most of the teachers there. God quickly elevated me to a place where I learned even more about myself as an educator, and I was able to learn from other educators. I was also able to teach my colleagues. Even though I was learning a lot and enjoying the position, I was not ready for it. I wanted to be back in the classroom. I wanted to be back with the students. I wanted to be able to apply what I was learning in my own classroom, with my own students. One thing I have learned about leadership is that you are respected more if you have actually been in the trenches. That's exactly where I wanted to be. Of course, when the enemy sees how joyful you have become, he tries to do anything possible to kill, steal, and destroy. What he did not know was that God had my back! I was told by the higher ups that they wanted me to go back into the classroom to get more classroom experience. Of course, there was more to the story than that, and initially I was hurt. But God! After some reflecting, I realized this was exactly what I wanted. It was not done in the right way, but God turned it around for my good. I became a sixth-grade English language arts teacher, and my classroom became the model classroom for the school.

If we take a look at Nehemiah, we can see that it took four months for his prayer to be answered. I am sure it seemed like forever to him. It took five years for me to finally become a classroom teacher. My plan was to become a second-grade teacher, shaping the lives of my students. God's perfect timing and plan for my life led me from an elementary interventionist, to a middle school interventionist, to a literacy coach, and finally a sixth-grade teacher. Had I not waited on God and trusted His plan for me, I would have missed out on so many experiences and lessons learned. God knows what He is doing, and He knows when to do it. We must learn to be patient, trust Him, and wait on Him.

I Surrender

"Mortals make elaborate plans, but God has the last word. Humans are satisfied with whatever looks good; God probes for what is good. Put God in charge of your work, then what you've planned will take place. God made everything with a place and purpose; even the wicked are included—but for judgment." -**Proverbs 16: 1-4 MSG**

"Their responsibility is to equip God's people to do his work and build up the church, the body of Christ." -**Ephesians 4:12 NLT**

"But by shifting our focus from what we do to what God does, don't we cancel out all our careful keeping of the rules and ways God commanded? Not at all. What happens, in fact, is that by putting that entire way of life in its proper place, we confirm it." -**Romans 3:31 MSG**

As I have stated previously, I used to be a planner. Every part of my life was planned. I was going to do this by this age, and that by that age. It was not until recently that I learned the true meaning of letting God guide my path. I finally got to the point where I surrendered. I was tired of making plans that fell through and feeling disappointed because of it. This was all my fault. I was claiming

God to be the head of my life, but I was trying to be in control of my life. I do not know why I thought that would work. I finally received the confirmation I had been desperately seeking. I had spent several months telling God that I turned all of my life over to Him. Prophetess Samantha called me one morning with a confirming word.

12/8/18

God says you are now fully aligned to His plan and His will and now He can do what He wants to do. You have completely turned over your plan, your vision, your discretion, your discernment, your time, your peace, your joy, your body, your mind, your will, your desire, to the Most High God, and because you have completely released what was once Tina J. Stukes, He can now do what He wants to do in your life.

Thank you, Lord! Have Your way! I surrender!

The time had finally come! 2019 was my year of alignment. So exactly what did that mean? It is funny how God literally gives you what you need in order to take the next steps in life. As I was pondering what was meant by alignment, I came across a live video by the very anointed Minister Adrienne Young. She was discussing what you should do once God gave you a word or words for the new year. The first thing was to research the word's definition, followed by synonyms, then antonyms. Researching the definition helped me to understand exactly what it meant to be aligned. After defining the word, the synonyms were to be turned into declarations. Finally, the antonyms are the things you pray against. God gave me two words and two phrases for 2019.

01/01/19

Alignment (n) - arrangement in a straight line or in correct or appropriate relative positions.

- a position of agreement or alliance

Eph. 4:12 – The word equipping is "katartizo" in the Greek and it means "alignment or to put a thing in its proper position. (Charisma News)

"Alignment increases your authority to function in Christ's Kingdom."

Synonyms (Declarations)

- I am being arranged by God to do His will.

- God is laying out the blueprint/roadmap for my life!

- I am in alliance, affiliating, and partnering with God!

- God is ordering my steps and positioning me for what is next.

- God is molding me into who He created me to be.

Antonyms – nonalignment

Shifting (adj) - changing, especially unpredictably

CHANGE!! MOVE!!

Romans 3: 31 MSG

Synonyms (Declarations)

- God is changing things around in my life.

- He is causing a mighty move upon my life.

Antonyms – immobility, motionless, halt, shutdown, termination

Because I finally let go of all my plans, God is able to do what He needs to do in my life. I have truly changed my way of thinking. I have no clue what my future career may be, but I have not tried to figure it out. God led to me create a blueprint for the future house I am to receive. I have no clue when I will get it, where it will be located, or how I am going to get it. All I know is that it was prophesied to me and God will handle the rest. After going through depression for the second time, I made the decision to be single for the rest of my life, even though my family was already prophesied to me. I made the decision to get into a relationship believing that man was my husband. It was my plan. I was already running behind on my timeline, but once again, I was wrong. After coming out of depression, I realized I had to put my plans and timelines to the side. I have no idea who my husband may be, when he will find me, or when we will start our lives together. I do know that all those things will happen in God's perfect timing. I no longer worry about them happening. Life is less stressful once you fully surrender everything to God. I was afraid to pay my tithes because I did not know if I would have enough money to pay all my bills. I would tell God He was my provider and I trust Him, but yet I was not showing it. Once I surrendered, I began to pay my tithes without worrying how my bills would get paid. I am not in control of my life, God is. Everything that happens in my life is much bigger than me. God has a plan and a purpose for it all. I wish it had not taken me this long to realize it.

I am Truly Blessed

*"For you bless the godly, O Lord; you surround them with your shield of love." -**Psalms 5:12 NLT***

Despite all my trials and tribulations, I am truly blessed. God has blessed me above and beyond anything I could ever imagine. I know the meaning of Psalm 5:12 and Ephesians 3:20. I have seen these verses manifest in my life on numerous occasions, and I am confident that they will continue to do so. God has made so many promises that have blown my mind before they even happened. I have learned not to limit Him because His blessings are greater, bigger, and better than anything I could ever think of. I can recall a time when my spiritual sister Samantha and I went for a drive. She took me to the middle of nowhere and showed me a house. She then said, "Think bigger!" This is just the first step. I know that I am so humble to the point where I am content with what I have, but I continuously learn not to limit God.

I know the favor of God follows me. It has shown its face so many times in my life. It was not until I built a strong relationship with God, and He surrounded me by some powerful and anointed people, that I knew what favor was. At the age of sixteen, I applied for my first job at Wendy's. I was terrified of having an interview, even though the manager was my best friend's mom. On the day of my interview, I went in not feeling prepared. She told me she was not feeling well so she was not going to interview me, but she was going to hire me. I know now that was the favor of God.

A few years later I was deciding on college. There were only two colleges I wanted to attend, which were South Carolina State University in Orangeburg, South Carolina, and Winthrop University in Rock Hill, South Carolina. I decided to go with Winthrop. It was the only school I applied to, and I was overjoyed once I received my acceptance letter. That was the favor of God. My junior year at Winthrop I wanted a job. I do not remember how I came across Lowe's Home Improvements in York, South Carolina, but the human resource manager attended Winthrop. I had gotten to know him in passing. I applied, went in for an interview, and the interview went terribly. I was not sure whether I was going to get the job, but I did! Once again, God's favor was upon me.

"Now all glory to God, who is able, through his mighty power at work within us, to accomplish infinitely more than we might ask or think." - **Ephesians 3:20 NLT**

While I was well into my career, I came to a point where I needed a change. I was physically, mentally, and emotionally tired. I was praying that God would show me my next steps. There were so many things I loved about my current school, but there were so many things I felt I also outgrew. I needed to experience something different to grow as an educator. One of my very good friends, Shanell Wilkes, was a teacher at the best middle school in Rock Hill, South Carolina (in my opinion.) I had heard so many positive things about the school and the principal. Of course, she got me interested in wanting to be a part of that community based on her experiences within one year of working at the school. She emailed the principal my resume months before I was even thinking about moving to a new school.

I remember the afternoon very clearly. I had just gotten home and was on the phone with my mortgage company. The call came through from a number that was unfamiliar to me. I do not answer calls from numbers I do not know, so I hit decline. I am going to say that once more, I HIT DECLINE. Normally, when you hit decline, it hangs up on the incoming call. Well, that was not the case. The phone hung up on my mortgage company. To my surprise, the principal was on the other end of the line.

"Hello?"

"Hello..."

"May I speak with Miss Tina Stukes."

"Speaking."

"Hi Miss Stukes, this is Norris Williams from Dutchman Creek Middle School."

"Oh, hi Dr. Williams, how are you?"

"I am well thanks. Miss Stukes, I have received your information, and I heard you are amazing!"

"Oh wow, that is a lot to live up to."

(laughs) "Are you considering moving schools next year?

"Yes I am!"

"Great, well look at your schedule and let's set up a time for an interview."

"Awesome! Thank you so much!"

"My pleasure, have a great evening."

Did that really just happen? Did I really receive a phone call for a job I did not apply for? God was definitely up to something. I went into my interview extremely confident and "blew it out of the water." I was offered the job in March, two months before the current school year ended. I was so excited, but it was definitely bittersweet. I was going to miss my Chester Middle School family, but I knew God had a plan and purpose in it all. It was time for me to get out of my comfort zone. I later came to know that my move was not just about getting out of my comfort zone. I was on an assignment.

The following February, I received another unexpected phone call. One of the ladies I obtained my master's degree with left public education to go teach at York Technical College. We had not spoken to each other in almost seven years. When I answered the phone, we briefly caught up and she asked if I would be interested in teaching a college level reading course. Apparently, the current professor needed to go out on medical leave, and they needed a replacement immediately. I was blown away.

My career goal was to teach in the K-12 classroom for at least ten years, then move to higher education. Here I was on year nine and my goal was manifesting. It is amazing how the devil will step in to try and steal your joy. After speaking with the department chair, I received the HR packet. While completing the packet, I noticed a stipulation that discussed how employees could not have student loans that were in default. Well, mine were in default. Instantly, I was going to let the devil have the victory. I was not going to go forward with the process. I was ashamed. How was I supposed to tell him my student loans were in default? I experienced a lot of warfare for a few days, but in the end, God showed me that I was not alone, and that He had the final say. I told the department chair my situation, he told me to continue the packet anyway while he communicated with Human Resources, and through the grace of God, I got the job! The enemy lost again!

Once that happened, I felt led to do a Facebook live to share my testimony. I had always kept my financial situation to myself, but I felt like someone else needed to know that they were not alone in the struggle. It is my belief that God brings us through situations for us to help others. The situations we face in life are not just about us. Someone needs to know that they are not the only one going through whatever they may be facing in order for them to make it through. Shortly after my live, I watched a video by Bishop T.D. Jakes that confirmed my belief. His words were:

"Nothing just happens. Whatever God has determined to happen will come to pass. And no devil in hell has ever been able to abort the purpose of God. Not once! Your mistakes were in His will. Your troubles were in HIs will. Your pain was in His will. God can preach more to you through the things you go through than He ever will through the sermons you hear."

That message WRECKED me! I needed to know that I was in the right place. I needed to know that I was doing the right things. I needed to know that God was allowing all this chaos in my life to happen for a reason, and this message showed me it was so. Every mistake I've ever made in my life was determined to happen by God. Any trouble I faced or will face in my life has been determined by God. All the pain I have endured and will endure has been pre-determined by God. The same stands true for you. It is not a question of will these things happen, but what will be our response?

It is so true that God can preach more to us when we go through things because that is when we naturally seek Him the most. I am guilty of sometimes "forgetting" about my Creator when things were going good in my life, but with spiritual growth came an unction to make room and time for Him always. God was working on me and using every aspect of my life to do so. I was no longer in that deep, dark place. I was starting to see the light!

Get in Your Quiet Place

"But when you pray, go away by yourself, shut the door behind you, and pray to your father in private. Then your Father, who sees everything, will reward you." -Matthew 6:6 NLT

"But Jesus Himself would often slip away to the wilderness and pray [in seclusion]."-Luke 5:16 AMP

There is something amazing about what happens when you spend time with God. I had never known the power of a prayer or war room until I got one myself. I was inspired to turn one of the rooms in my house into my war room after watching the movie that was inspired by Priscilla Shirer. She is a wonderful person to follow for spiritual guidance.

I love to sit in my war room and just read my Bible and talk to God. It is amazing how I can feel His presence. The best part is listening. I have had so many downloads from just sitting quiet and yielding to His voice. I always stop and welcome Him in. I've received deliverance in that room. I've seen breakthroughs in that room. Something happens when I turn on Nathaniel Coe's prophetic soaking music. I get laid out every time!

I can remember times when I was sitting in my war room praying for God to show me this or show me that. Once I got quiet and just waited, I received the downloads. There was a time when I was stuck with writing this book. I thought maybe I was finished. While I was quietly sitting in my war room, He downloaded an entire chapter for me to write. I have gotten the blueprint to my house I am going to build. I have no clue about blueprints. I don't even know if it is aligned correctly, but I know that house will not be built on anything I can do on my own. I have no idea how God is going to work it out, but I know He will.

I have started a business in my war room. A BUSINESS! God has given me several prophecies about my business. I do not know what I am doing. I simply go into my war room, ask Him to show me, and He does the rest.

I once had a client to ask me how I planned to grow my business. My response was simple, "It's not my plan, it's God's plan. He gave me the prophecy. I honestly don't know what I'm doing. I just act in obedience. The website is almost finished, business cards are about to be reprinted, LLC is in the works, and I'm already networking. My business is built on the promises of God. Every shirt I've made for you has been prayed over. I have an expectation on my products.

That's another occurrence that happened in my war room. I told God that I did not want to just make products. I want my products to shift atmospheres, change mindsets, bring breakthroughs and deliverance, and turn nonbelievers into believers. I told God that I have an expectancy on my products, and at that point I knew that I was entering the marketplace ministry. Amazing things happen when you get quiet and talk to God. Astounding things happen when you yield and listen to God.

"But don't just listen to God's word. You must do what it says. Otherwise, you are only fooling yourselves. For if you listen to the word and don't obey, it is like glancing at your face in a mirror." -James 1:22-23 **NLT**

The other part of getting into your quiet place is obeying. This verse is a great depiction of why you can't just listen to God's word. You cannot simply read the Word. You must do what it says. You can get quiet all day long, get as many downloads as you want, but if you do not do what God says, it is all for nothing.

Had I not been obedient, I would have not written this book. Had I not listened to what God told me to do, I would not have a business. Had I not been obedient, I would not have been on the spiritual level I am today.

God is amazing. He gives us what we need. Every answer is in the Word. He will provide every detail. Our job is to get quiet, listen, yield, and obey. If you need healing, go to God. If you need a breakthrough, go to God. If you need deliverance, go to God. If you need a financial blessing, go to God. If you need provision, go to God. Anything you need, you can get from God. I am a living witness to this. Get in your quiet place, talk with Him, and obey His commands.

So How Did Writing Save My Life?

*"Having carefully investigated everything from the beginning, I also have decided to write an accurate account for you, most honorable Theophilus, so you can be certain of the truth of everything you were taught." -**Luke** 1:3-4 **NLT***

I've always loved to write. As a middle school and high school student, I wrote letters to my friends all the time. My best friend and I wrote letters to each other just about every day. We even created a coded alphabet. I also wrote music and poetry. Writing was my way of venting. My joy for writing accelerated in middle school. I wrote a narrative and my teacher told me I had "voice." That simple piece of feedback encouraged and inspired me to write more.

Writing became my way of venting and dealing with situations. I wasn't much of a talker, so I did not express myself to my family and friends. I held everything in, but I began to write about the things that bothered me and the things I did not want to share with anyone. I have several journals still at my parents' house now. I would sit in my room and write for hours.

However, my first writing class in college changed my perspective of writing. I began to hate it. Because I had always received positive feedback on my writing, I did not handle getting negative feedback well. Every paper I ever wrote in that class was never good enough. Something was always wrong, even after revisions. I remember having a conversation with my aunt about my frustrations in the class and how I did not know what to do to improve my writing. Her response was, "She does not understand your style of writing."

That stuck with me after I became a teacher. It gave me a different view of how to grade the writing of my students. Yet still, my love for writing slowly faded away. Even after passing the writing class that was taught by the "hardest writing professor" at Winthrop University, I lost my desire to write. Eventually I completely stopped. Due to the fact that I did not have writing as my outlet, I think that partially led to my depression after the death of my grandmother. Reflecting back on the situation, I had not gotten to the point where I opened up to God about what I was going through before I stopped writing. I did not know how to allow Him to comfort me and speak to me.

Years later, I slowly began journaling again when I got into Bible study. Minister Adrienne Young talked about the different things she wrote in her journal, and I got inspired. I began to write down every prophetic word that was spoken to me, and different insights I received while reading and meditating on God's word. That year I was literally gifted with five journals on several different occasions. I took that as a sign to begin writing again. That was one of the best decisions I could have ever made.

Writing and spending time in God's presence helped me get through my second round with depression. It was the first summer since I was a teacher that I did not work. I spent the entire summer on the couch reading my Bible, praying, writing in my journal, and crying out to God. I just wanted to "see the light at the end of the tunnel." I wanted that situation to be over. I wanted to be filled with joy again, but all I felt was sorrow. It was as if a heavy cloud of sadness followed me everywhere I went.

Meanwhile, I acted as if everything was fine around my family and friends. I was asking God to heal my broken heart, to show me what was next for my life, to help me make it through this situation that I brought on myself. Life is so much easier when we follow God's purpose and plan for our lives. Being able to audibly express my feelings to God, as well as write about them brought me out of a horrible state.

I can look back through my journals and see my growth. I can look back through my journals and document my journey. I can look back through my journals and thank God for what I've been through. I can look back through my journals and thank God for where He's taking me. I can continue to write to inspire others. I can continue to write to give God the glory for my story. I can continue to write for someone to see they are not in the fight alone. I'm grateful for all that I have endured, but most of all, I am grateful that God has allowed me to write to be a blessing to others, to show others how wonderful He is, and to be an inspiration to everyone on their spiritual journey. I am filled with gratitude that writing to God saved my life.

Declarations and Affirmations

*"You will also decide and decree a thing, and it will be established for you; And the light [of God's favor] will shine upon your ways."***-Job 22:28 AMP**

One of the most powerful things I have learned on my spiritual journey is to write out declarations and affirmations and to speak them over my life until they manifest. Even though I am listing declarations and affirmations, I encourage you to partner with God and write your own. Speak them over your life every day. I used to write mine on sticky notes and put them on the mirror in my bathroom. Now, I write them in my journals. Choose what works best for you, but do not stop declaring and decreeing until you receive the manifestation.

I declare and decree that I will have the joy of the Lord in my heart.

I declare and decree that I will have peace all the days of my life.

I declare and decree that God's favor is upon my life.

I declare and decree that goodness and mercy shall follow me.

I will continue to gain knowledge and wisdom on my spiritual journey.

I will continue to grow closer to God.

I am in partnership with God and an heir to the kingdom.

My words have power, I will have what I say.

About the Author

Born in Manning, South Carolina, Tina J. Pearson attended Winthrop University where she obtained her bachelor's degree in Elementary Education and master's degree in Literacy. She is currently enrolled at Grand Canyon University working towards a master's degree in Mental Health Counseling with a focus on Christian Ministry. Tina has been an educator for 12 years. She is the owner of T3 Creations and More, LLC and Co-Founder of The Growth Experience, an online community that helps others grow through what they go through.

Tina enjoys traveling, reading, journaling, and spending time with family. Her desire is to teach the world about the goodness of God and to help those battling anxiety and depression.

CPSIA information can be obtained
at www.ICGtesting.com
Printed in the USA
BVHW050845290721
613098BV00013B/1498

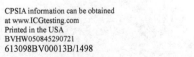